I0955776

Raise Your Child's Self-Esteem!

99

Easy Things to Do

Text copyright © 2000 by Nancy Krulik.
Illustrations copyright © 2000 by Scholastic Inc.
All rights reserved. Published by Scholastic Inc.
SCHOLASTIC, CARTWHEEL BOOKS and associated logos
are trademarks and/or registered trademarks of Scholastic Inc.

No part of this publication may be reproduced, or stored in a retrieval system,
or transmitted in any form or by any means, electronic, mechanical, photo-
copying, recording, or otherwise, without written permission of the publisher.
For information regarding permission, write to Scholastic Inc., Attention:
Permissions Department, 555 Broadway, New York, NY 10012.

Library of Congress Cataloging-in-Publication Data available

ISBN: 0-439-19279-X

10 9 8 7 6 5 4 3 2 1   00 01 02 03 04

Printed in the U.S.A.   23
First printing, September 2000

Raise Your Child's Self-Esteem!

99

Easy Things to Do

by Nancy Krulik
Illustrations by Amanda Haley

SCHOLASTIC INC.

New York   Toronto   London   Auckland   Sydney
Mexico City   New Delhi   Hong Kong

*This book is dedicated
to my parents, Gladys and Steve,
for obvious reasons.*

Introduction

If there's one singular message in this book, it is this: Take the time to show your children how wonderful, unique, and special they are. Be there for them through the good and the bad. Be their cheerleader, teacher, and confidante. And show them that there is nothing you would rather do than be with them.

Self-esteem isn't something you're born with. In some ways, it's something you're given, like a gift. When children are very young, they develop much of their sense of self-worth by studying how others perceive them. If children only receive negative reinforcement, they won't think much of themselves. But if they get praise and encouragement often enough, they begin to develop a sense of pride in themselves that will sustain them for the rest of their lives.

Every child is special. Each one has unique talents and abilities that set him or her apart from everyone else. It's our job as parents to make sure that our children know just how remarkable they are. If they grow up filled with self-esteem, they will have the courage and confidence to go out into the world and try new things, to respect other people's ideas, and to face challenges with a sense that they can do anything they put their minds to.

And in the end, isn't that what parenting is all about?

Grow
Together

1

Tell your child you love him at least once a day.

2

Take your child's feelings seriously.
Try not to say she'll "grow out of it,"
or that it's "not that bad."

3

Let your child know it's okay to make mistakes. Admit your own.

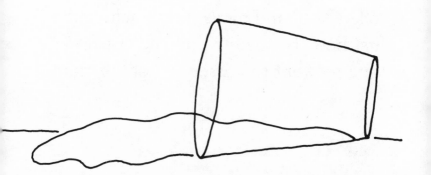

4

Make a board game about your child's life. Each space on the board can mark an accomplishment your child has made since he was born. Start at the beginning, with the first time he smiled or when he rolled over, and move on to include the first book he read to you and the first time he went to nursery school or camp.

5

Laugh at your child's jokes—even when you don't get them.

6

Praise your child's efforts, without worrying about the results.

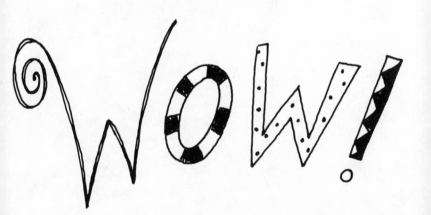

7

Take your child's picture each year on the first day of school. Don't forget to look back to see how much he's grown.

8

Encourage your child to ask questions.
Research the answers together.

9

Teach your child that "can't" is not forever. With a little hard work, your child will learn a new skill, and turn "I can't" into "I can."

10

Resist the urge to say "I told you so."

Pay attention to your child's random acts of kindness, and be sure to thank her for them.

Get duplicates made of your next roll of family photographs. Then use them to play a memory game with your child. To play, turn all of the photos facedown, and take turns trying to guess where the matches are. If your child guesses correctly, he gets to put those pictures in his own pile. If not, turn the pictures over again and keep playing. When all of the photos are gone, the player with the most matches wins.

Don't treat all of your children exactly alike. Each one has different needs.

14

Create a crystal ball collage. Let your child fill it with pictures and stories about what he hopes his future will be.

15

Pull out a photo album filled with your child's baby pictures. Tell him stories about when he was a baby. It will be a special trip down memory lane for both of you.

16

Talk out your disagreements with your child. If you give her the silent treatment now, she's liable to give it back to you later.

17

Don't let your child go to bed angry
with you—or thinking that you are
angry with him.

18

Teach your child that all people are entitled to their own points of view. Respect that your child has his own point of view, too.

Spot for President
woof!

19

Keep your child's secrets—unless keeping them will be harmful to her well-being.

Always say good-bye before you leave.
Sneaking away will make your child
distrustful.

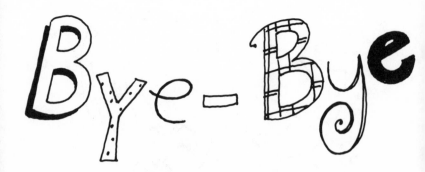

21

Let your child cry if he needs to. There's no need for him to take things like a grown-up. Remember, he's only a kid.

22

Start an "I Can" can. Ask your child to decorate an old coffee can with stickers, construction paper, and crayons. Every time your child masters a new skill, write it on a slip of paper and put it in the can. Check on the contents of the can from time to time, so your child can see how much she's learned.

23

Make a feelings chart with your child. List all the emotions your child can think of on a big piece of paper. Each day, ask your child to tape her picture next to the way she feels. Talk about what makes her feel that way.

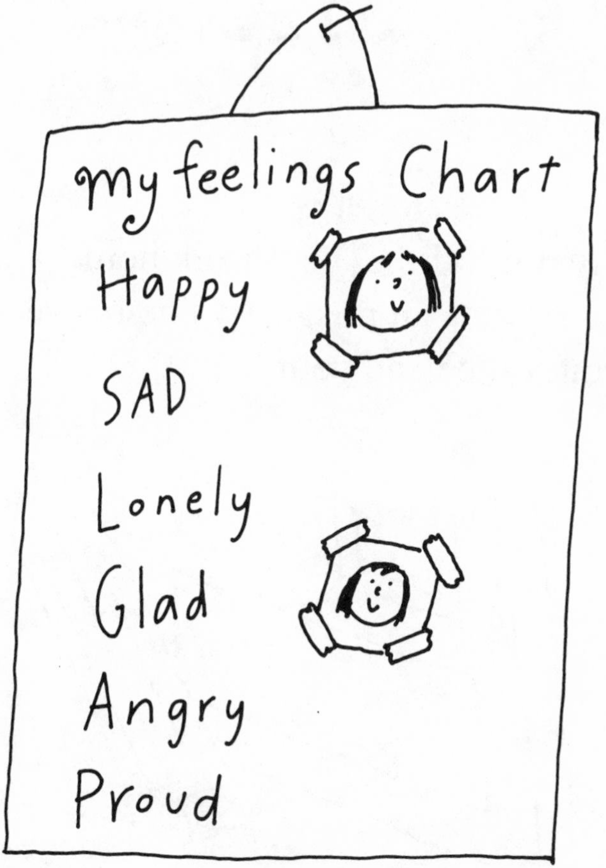
my feelings Chart
Happy
SAD
Lonely
Glad
Angry
Proud

24

Try not to bring your work home with you. Draw an imaginary line between your office and your home.

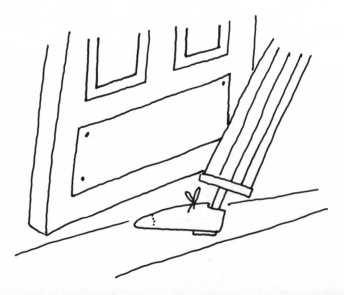

25

Wear your child's picture in a locket around your neck, or carry a wallet-sized snapshot wherever you go.

Children

First

26

Go for a walk and write a poem about your neighborhood.

27

Let your child push the button in the elevator. If you don't have an elevator, allow your child to play doorman for you—you might even want to give her the keys and let her turn the lock!

Let your child tie *your* shoes and zip *your* jacket for a change.

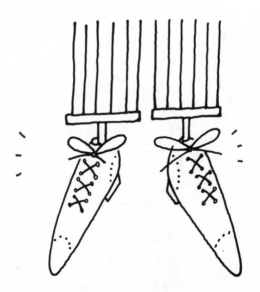

29

Send care packages to sleep-away camp.
Remember to include a special note
from you.

30

Take a day off to go along on your child's class field trip.

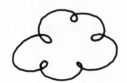

31

Let your child have an extra dessert once in a while.

32

Listen to your child's favorite CD—and try to like the music. You might even find yourself singing along one day.

33

Have the sleepover at your house sometimes. And to make your sleepover just a little more special, why not give it a theme, like a safari! Ask the children to wear animal pajamas. Have them eat animal crackers and roar like lions before they go to bed.

34

Have a make-believe tea party together.
Allow your child to be the one who pours.

35

Let your child record the message on the family answering machine.

36

When it's holiday time, let your child sign his name first on your family's greeting cards.

37

Have your child make the wrapping paper when you give a gift to a family friend or relative. All she'll need is a big piece of blank paper, some markers, and lots of imagination.

38

Play school together, and let your child be the teacher. You'll be surprised at how much you both will learn.

39

Spruce up her backpack with fabric paints.

40

Set up a still life and spend some time drawing it together.

41

Just once, let your child be the first one on the block to have something.

42

Get your child his own magazine subscription.

43

Ask your child to come up with a new family tradition. Try to keep up the tradition at least once a month.

Play office at your home. Let your child
be the boss!

MEMO

To: Jill
From: mommy
Date: Today
Re: I Love You!

45

Create a "digging spot" in your backyard
for your child. Make it a special place
where she can dig as big a hole as she
possibly can, make mud pies, and just
generally get dirty.

46

Keep the Earth clean for your child.
Teach him to recycle.

Creative
Play

47

Make and paint a wooden birdfeeder together. Then sit and watch from the window as the birds fly over to enjoy your efforts.

Home
Sweet
Home

48

Have a circus day at home. Use face paints to turn you and your child into clowns. Then take turns taming "wild" stuffed animals, walking across masking tape highwires (that are on the floor, of course), and eating circus treats like peanuts and popcorn.

49

Buy blank note cards and decorate them together. Use them as birthday cards, get-well cards, or just for fun!

50

Sit down on a newspaper-covered floor with your child and try finger painting with your toes.

51

Work together to make the world's scariest, funniest, or most creative Halloween costume ever!

52

Work together to build a robot out of small interlocking blocks. Then talk about the things your child wishes her new robot could do for her.

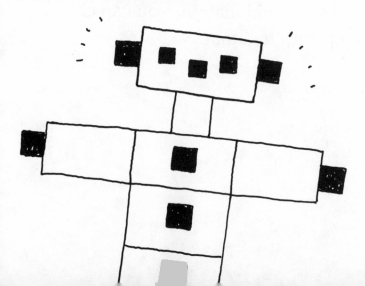

53

Spend an afternoon drawing crazy animals with your child. Use the wings of a bird, the tail of a tiger, the feet of a pig. See how many wacky combinations you can come up with together.

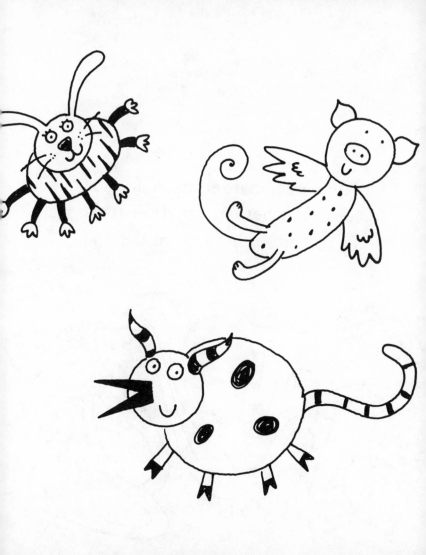

54

Create a personalized maze for your child to solve. Put her baby picture at the start and a picture of her now at the end.

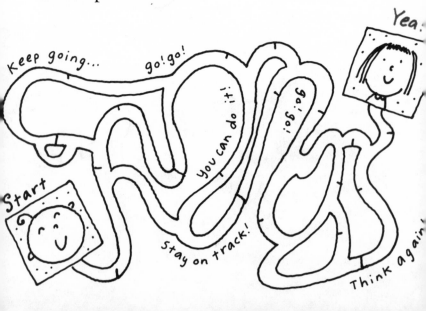

55

Bake warm bread together on a cold, snowy day.

56

Use permanent markers to decorate
T-shirts for each other. Be sure to wear
the shirt your child makes for you.

57

Spend an afternoon making friendship bracelets for each other.

58

Help your child create his own security blanket. Give him a piece of an old sheet and some markers. Encourage him to draw something that makes him happy.

59

Cut your child's lunch sandwiches into fun shapes. Use cookie cutters to make stars, flowers, and leaves.

60

Create a miniature golf course in your living room or backyard. Cut out the bottom of an oatmeal container to make a tunnel. Use a Hula Hoop™ to create a sandpit. Use Frisbees™ to mark off a curved fairway. A broomstick makes a fine golf club. When you're all set up, tee off with your child.

61

Spend the day making bead projects. You can use store-bought beads, make your own beads from clay, or just string macaroni of different shapes and sizes.

62

Collect and dry flowers together.
Use the dried flowers to decorate
your home.

63

Make holiday decorations with your child. After the festivities are over, pack them away carefully and be sure to bring them out again next year.

64

Make sock puppets together. You can use buttons for eyes, felt for mouths, and yarn for hair. Use your puppets to put on a parent-child puppet show.

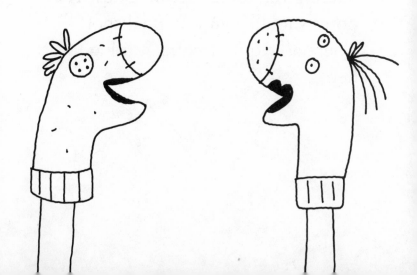

Have a scavenger hunt in your home. If your child is already reading, leave riddles around the house that will take her from place to place. If she isn't reading yet, leave picture clues. The notes should lead to a final spot—where a favorite treat is waiting for her.

go to
Look under
find the
to the
there in
the above
for the
next big Clue!

66

Go to the park and find some interesting rocks. Then go home and paint them.

67

Tell a favorite fairy tale, but replace the main character's name with your child's. Doesn't "Sam and the Beanstalk" have a nice ring to it? How about "Phoebe and the Three Bears"?

68

Make a personalized jigsaw puzzle for your child. Glue your favorite picture of the two of you together to a piece of sturdy cardboard. Cut the cardboard into jigsaw-puzzle pieces, and let her solve the puzzle.

69

Put together a special cookbook of all your child's favorite snacks and meals. Let your child illustrate it. Try making some of the recipes together.

70

Work together to decorate gingerbread cookies that look like your child.

71

Work together to make a detailed map of your neighborhood. Be sure to include your child's favorite places—like candy stores, swimming pools, the greatest sledding hill, and his best friend's house. Then go outside and follow the map!

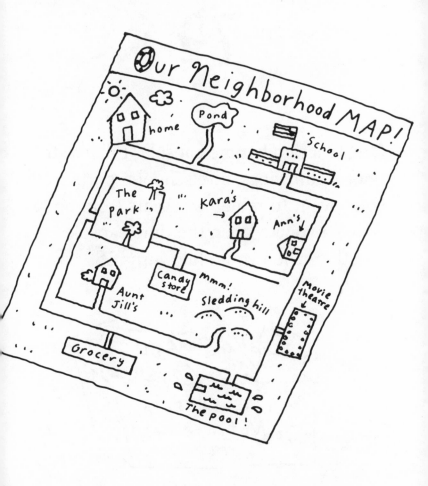

72

Create a family time capsule. Fill it with photos, drawings, and school reports you'll want to remember years from now. Make a vow to open the time capsule together when your child turns 18.

73

Draw a family comic strip together. Include caricatures of family members and place funny sayings in the word balloons above their heads.

74

Draw portraits of each other. Hang them in a special family art gallery.

75

Make paper snowflakes together and hang them in your windows. Be sure to tell your child that no two snowflakes are the same—which makes each one special, just like him.

Together
Time

76

Set aside a special talking time every day, when you can discuss the day's events. Keep this time sacred—no TV shows or telephone calls can interrupt.

77

Go down the big slide holding your child between your legs. Maybe the next time she won't be afraid to go by herself.

Instead of asking your child how school was, try asking him to tell you three great things he did that day. You're sure to love the answers you receive!

79

While you're both waiting in a restaurant, take the time to play I'm Thinking of an Animal. Have your child ask yes or no questions until she can guess what animal you have in mind. Then reverse roles.

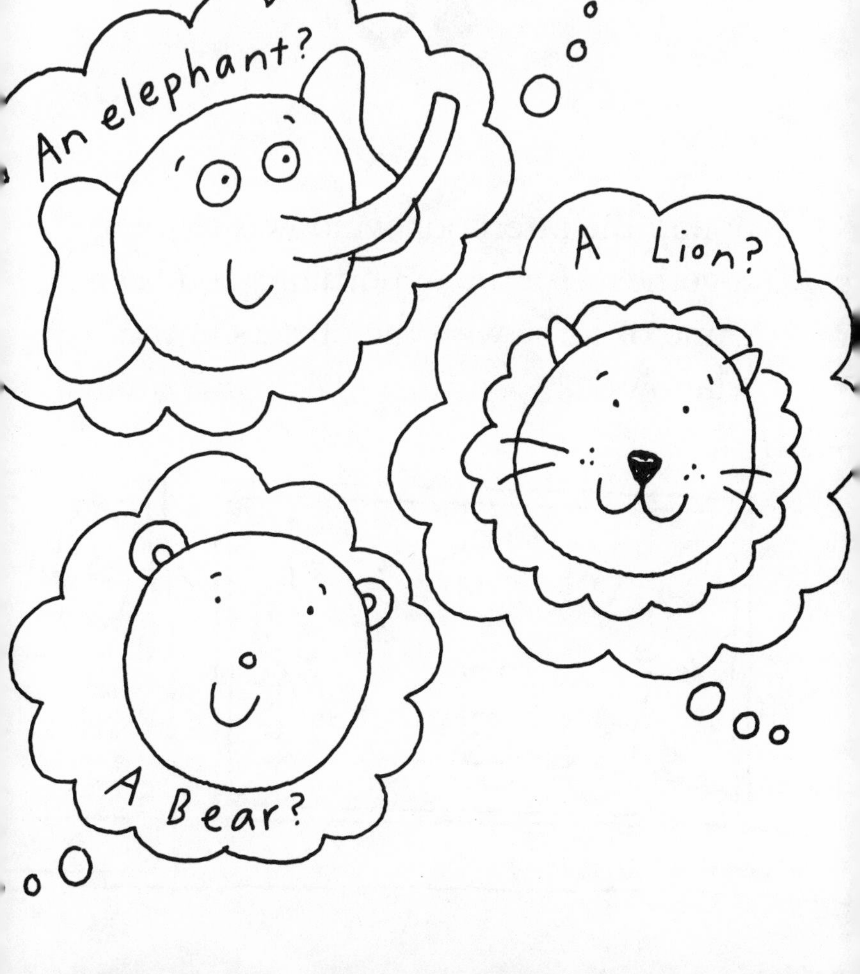
An elephant?
A Lion?
A Bear?

80

Spend the afternoon window-shopping together. Use the opportunity to play a game of I Spy with the objects in the windows.

81

Rake the leaves with your child.
Then jump in the pile together.

82

Create a secret language only you and your child can understand.

HLOVEAPPOVEYOVE

83

Sit together on a park bench and watch the world go by.

84

Learn to play your child's favorite
CD-ROM game.

85

Share a banana split—and let your child
pick the toppings.

86

Play rhyming games as you walk to school or the playground. Pick a word and see how many others you can find that rhyme with that word. Silly, made-up words count, too.

Mat

Fat

Cat

Rat

that

bAt

SLUGGER

SAT

Gnat

hat

87

Teach your child the lullabies you sang to him when he was a baby.

88

Work together to make up new words to "Twinkle, Twinkle, Little Star." Be sure to permanently record your version on tape for posterity.

Scurry, scurry, Little Mouse

89

Take a trip to a local children's museum.

90

Learn a new skill along with your child. Start piano lessons together. Join a parent-child basketball clinic. Learn a foreign language as a team.

91

Ride a merry-go-round with your child.
Sit on the horse right next to his.

92

Use your video camera to make a commercial together.

93

Build a snowman together.

94

Have a mug of hot cocoa ready when your child comes in from playing in the snow.

95

Spend New Year's Eve at home as a family, and let your child try to stay up until midnight.

96

Work together to build a really huge
sand castle at the beach.

Play family trivia. Use index cards to write down little bits of information about your child and the rest of the family. Then ask each other questions, and see who knows the most.

Our family Trivia

You were born at 2:02 am!

98

Have a campout on your living room floor. Snuggle into sleeping bags, watch movies, and eat popcorn together.

99

Sing in the rain with your child—and make really big splashes in the puddles.